# PICK THE RIGHT PLACE

## RYAN ERISMAN

# CONTENTS

# INTRODUCTION

52% of my readers say that one of their greatest fears about retirement is moving to the wrong place.

That's second only to not having enough assets or income.

Imagine if there was a resource you could access whenever you wanted, that included a logically organized system to walk you step-by-step through the process of figuring out where to retire, and guiding you through all the steps required to actually make it a reality.

That would be great right?

Well I'm here today to tell you that such a thing does exist and you're holding it in your hands.

You've followed systems to advance in your career and profession.

You've followed systems to save those hard earned dollars to be able to live wherever you want in retirement.

But nobody has put together a system to help you through the process of figuring out the best place for YOU.

Until now.

For years readers just like you have allowed me to help them discover the information they need to make educated decisions about the best places to retire and achieve their retirement dreams.

Whether it's been through my "for Boomers" family of books and websites like *Florida for Boomers*, through my best-selling book *Inside the Bubble* about The Villages, I've helped thousands of people navigate this process.

From years of hearing my readers' thoughts, worries and concerns, it became clear that there was a need for a more organized and deeply supported training program to help them allay their greatest fear of moving to the wrong place.

Based on the hundreds of conversations with people just like yourself, I've taken years of questions, answers, and resources shared and organized them into a logical system for all to use and benefit from.

You could try and figure this all out yourself.

And you know what? With a couple hundred hours of research and lots of trial and error, you could probably do it.

Or you could take the shortcut.

You see, I spent the last 10 years helping other people figure out where to retire, and I'm going to share everything I know inside this book.

As John C Maxwell said,

"It's said that a wise person learns from his mistakes. A wiser one learns from others' mistakes. But the wisest person of all learns from others's successes."

Let's jump right in!

# CHAPTER 1
## CHOOSING A LOCATION

C hoosing an area in which to live can be one of the most difficult decisions you ever have to make. There are many great choices available to you.

But you can use the tips in this book to narrow your choices down and eventually make a final decision on a place that fits your lifestyle and budget, suits your housing needs and desires, and that you'll love for years to come.

### Getting Started

These days, the best place to start your search is online. Visit the websites of the local newspapers for the cities, towns, or areas you are investigating and do some general exploring and reading.

You can often find information on the history of an area, photo tours and sometimes "virtual" video tours. Don't forget to scan the real estate classifieds to get a feel for home prices in the area. It will also be helpful to read some local articles and editorials. These can give you a sense of the feel of an area, and reveal items of interest or concern for the local residents.

Radio and TV news stations also have some excellent resources on their websites. Radio stations can be especially helpful for finding information in line with your interests. For example, a community calendar for a country music station might list events that would appeal to their typical listener. These events would be different than events that might interest an oldies or easy listening crowd.

Next, visit the websites of the area chambers of commerce and request an information package. The information packages will usually include a brochure on the area filled with advertisements for local businesses, information on annual events, a guide to local history, and usually a map of the area. These information packages used to be printed and mailed but these days they are more likely to be delivered in a digital format.

In addition, request information from some new home builders and communities in the area, to see if the types of houses they offer appeal to your wants and needs.

If the area seems like it might meet your requirements, go to the next step.

**Government**

Visit the website of the local government. By the looks of things, are they up-to-date technologically? Read through official statements and press releases you may find. What are the taxes like in the area? Is the government being wise and prudent in their spending, or does it seem like they are plundering windfalls from property tax increases? These are all not easily answered questions but with a little research you can get a feel for what some of the answers might be.

**Home Prices**

To get a general feel for what the prices of homes are in the area in which you are looking, visit sites like Realtor.com or Zillow.com. They will show you all the homes listed in the city or zip code that you specify. Enter your required number of bedrooms and bathrooms as well as your price range and see which homes come up as a result.

**Make a Visit**

Now that you've gathered a bunch of information on places you think might interest you, it's time to make a visit.

When you visit an area, especially one you've never been to before, there are certain things you'll want to look for to help you decide if this is an area you might like to live in.

Drive through some different parts of the local area. As you are driving, are you seeing restaurants, businesses, shopping centers and so forth that look appealing to you and that match your ideal lifestyle?

Stop in at some different establishments like restaurants or shopping malls and take a look around. Ask people you come in contact with what they like or don't like about the area. See if they have any recommendations of places to look for homes or any other relevant information they are willing to share.

**Drive Through Some Neighborhoods**

Take a detour off the main roads and into some residential

neighborhoods. Are the homes what you expected? Are people's yards well maintained?

Visit some of the new communities and model homes in the area or take a tour of some resale homes that you've arranged to see ahead of time with your real estate agent.

**Facilities and Services**

Look for the amenities that are important to you. Are there libraries nearby and are they up to date? What about medical facilities? Check to make sure an area's cultural activities, recreation facilities, beaches and parks, golf courses, and whatever else is important to you are available at a level that will fit your needs and desires.

Make a list of your current weekly activities (garden club, rotary, church, etc.) and be sure that the area you choose provides you the opportunities to continue to do what you enjoy.

# CHAPTER 2
# LOCATION PREFERENCES

Decide which of the following location preferences are most important to you in the different categories below. If it helps you figure out what's most/least important, rate each item on a scale of 0-10, with 0 being "Highly Undesirable" and 10 being "Highly Desirable".

**Geographical Preferences**

Do you want to live near or at the beach?

Do you want to live in a city/urban environment?

Do you want to live in a small town?

Do you want to live near or on a lake?

Do you want to live near or on a river?

Do you want to live in the desert?

Do you want to live on a farm or ranch?

Do you want to live in the mountains?

Do you want to live in a college town?

Are there any other Geographic Preferences that come to mind for you?

**Weather Preferences**

Do you want to live somewhere with all four seasons?

Do you want to live somewhere with mostly warm weather and no seasons?

Do you want to live somewhere with lots of snow?

Do you want to live somewhere with lots of rainy days?

Do you want to live somewhere with dry weather?

Do you want to live somewhere with mostly sunny days?

Do you want to live somewhere with low humidity?

Do you want to live somewhere with little pollen/allergy issues?

Are there any other Weather Preferences that come to mind for you:

**Amenity Preferences**

Do you want to live near great restaurants?

Do you want to live near great shopping?

Do you want to live near a farmer's market?

Do you want to live near a movie theater?

Do you want to live near a performing arts center?

Do you want to live near museums and/or art galleries?

Do you want to live near college or professional sports venues?

Do you want to live near a great hospital and medical facilities?

Do you want to live near a library or bookstore?

Do you want to live on or near a golf course?

Do you want to live near hiking/skiing/biking trails?

Do you want to live near an airport or train station?

Do you want to live near a cruise port?

Are there any other Amenity Preferences that come to mind for you?

**Family and Social Preferences**

Do you want to live near your children and/or grandchildren?

Do you want to live near your aging parents?

Do you want to live near your siblings?

Do you want to live near people your age?

Do you want to live near people of all ages?

Do you want to live near people culturally and/or politically like you?

Do you want to live near people different from you?

• • •

Are there any other Family and Social Preferences that come to mind for you?


After completing this exercise, you've hopefully developed some rough ideas of what you want your future lifestyle to look and feel like. You probably even have a good idea about what part of the country you'd like to live in.


Congratulations, there is more work to be done, but you are well on your way!

# CHAPTER 3
# COST OF LIVING

I n this chapter, we're going to discuss cost of living, which is a topic on everybody's mind when they're moving to a new place.

Lots of people who move to other states for retirement or maybe just a new place within their own state have planned and saved for the move for years, if not decades.

It's no surprise that some are reluctant to pull the trigger until they have a more complete understanding of what their cost of living will be. You don't want to end up somewhere, and then a few years down the road figure out that you really couldn't afford it, and you're watching your retirement savings deplete at a much faster rate than you ever thought it would.

What all do you need to be thinking about?

Now, things like mortgage or rent costs, homeowner's insurance, real estate taxes and the like are all pretty obvious, and they're pretty easy to get a handle on. But what some people forget to include and also struggle to get an accurate fix on are what their everyday expenses in a new location, like groceries, eating out, utilities, and so on, will be.

Where do you find the numbers for this information? Lately I've been turning to the website BestPlaces.net. For just about every major city in the country, BestPlaces provides a "cost of living index".

What is a "cost of living index"? According to their website:

"A cost of living index allows you to compare what it costs to live in one place against another, revealing how far your money will go in different areas. Scores are presented in relation to the national average of 100. If a place's COL index is below 100, it's cheaper than the national average. If it's over 100, it's more expensive than the national average.

For example, a cost of living index of 130 means it costs 30% more to live there as compared to the national average (130-100=30). If you perform the same calculation with a cost of index below the national average of 100, you'll get a negative number showing how much money you'll save. So, in a place with a COL of 85, that means it costs 15% less to live there than the national average (85-100=-15)."

That sounds great and all, but how do they get their data and come up with the index?

"The BestPlaces cost of living index is the most accurate and complete available because we add many new categories to the current and historical systems. We start with ACCRA's 100-as-national-average model adopted by the Council for Community and Economic Research (C2ER) in 1968, then update and expand it to include 21st-century consumer spending preferences and expenditure types.

Using sophisticated modeling techniques, our BestPlaces analysis expands the geographic scope of our Cost of Living Indexes down to the zip code level, covering every county, city, and metro area in the United States.

The BestPlaces cost of living score includes housing prices for renters or homeowners, utilities (electric, natural gas, oil), healthcare costs (premiums and common surgeries), entertainment costs, transportation expenses (vehicle insurance and registration fees, gas prices and commuting costs, vehicle depreciation), food prices (meat, dairy, ready-to-eat, and more), child care (for both infants and toddlers, at home and away from home), and taxes (income, property, sales, motor vehicle)."

One of the site's most useful features is the ability to compare any one of these metrics between two cities.

Say, for instance, you're considering a move from Boston, Massachusetts to Jacksonville, Florida. If you plug those two cities into the cost of living comparison tool, you'll find that housing costs in Jacksonville are about 70% lower than in Boston. Food and grocery prices are about 11% lower, and utilities are about 12% lower.

*The figures in in the above scenario are what they were when I first checked while writing this book and will likely change by the time you read it, but you get the gist.*

Now, is this site a perfect solution? No. For one thing, it's hard to tell how often the data gets updated, which is important considering how quickly the prices of some things are changing in recent years.

Another drawback to all websites like this is that they aren't able to account for your individual habits, tastes, and preferences. Your actual numbers may vary from what they show you, but if you use it as intended, which is as a general rule of thumb, BestPlaces should prove to be a big help in figuring out what your cost of living will be like across various cities.

# CHAPTER 4
## MAKING THE MOST OF YOUR RESEARCH TRIPS

Once you narrow down your list of places that you might want to spend your retirement years, of the next steps is to begin visiting the different places and communities in them to explore which one might be the best option for your new home.

Remember, you're looking for the perfect combination of location, people and housing for your needs, and there are more than a few options to pick from. This means that you're going to have to do some serious research in order to determine exactly which community is the best fit for you and your family.

With so many different criteria to evaluate and so many different options available, it's important to make every minute count on your research trips during the community shopping phase.

With that in mind, here are some simple tips to help you

focus your time while on your research trips. You'll likely have a fairly limited amount of time to explore each of your options. It is understandable that you'll want to get the most out of every minute you spend community shopping and cram as many communities into your trip as possible.

But rushing through each community visit is not going to get you the results you're looking for. It's a far better idea to visit fewer communities and take your time exploring each one than it is to rush through a large number of communities. In order to truly assess whether a particular community is right for you, you need to really dig in and get to know all the details of that community.

One of the most important things that I think people can do when they visit different communities is to talk to as many current residents as possible. Now, starting conversations with total strangers about their lifestyles might not be something you're comfortable with, but if you force yourself to do so, you'll find a wealth of information that's available to you, absolutely free.

What do they like about their houses? What do they like about their amenities? Do they like the builder and the developer? Why or why not? I think you'll find most people are a pretty open book, and will be more than happy to share their experiences to help you out.

And don't just focus on residents within a particular community. It's a good idea to ask people you come in contact with outside of the community, whether that's in restaurants or store, what their impression of the community you're considering is.

One mistake I see people make on their research trip is they go in with a budget in mind, but halfway through they've thrown that budget right out the window.

You won't be doing yourself any favors by wasting time looking at houses that are priced well above your realistic price range. Yes, there are some amazing houses in many of the communities you'll be exploring, and it's easy to get sucked in to looking at all of them, no matter how grand or out of your price range they are.

But this, not surprisingly, can take up a lot of time, time that's ultimately wasted if these places aren't near your budget, so your focus should always be on the houses, condos or villas you might actually consider buying.

One of the fun things about community research trips is that it can feel like you're on vacation, so the tendency is to eat at the best restaurants, do all the fun activities, and just throw caution to the wind as far as real life is concerned.

I'm not saying you can't do any of that, or have any fun, but once you become a permanent resident of a particular community, you probably won't be going out for fancy dinners every night, or packing your day with fun activities.

So when you're community shopping, you should spend some time exploring the more reasonably priced restaurants, and more everyday activities so you can get a better feel for what your everyday life will be like in each community.

When you're shopping for the perfect community with a limited amount of time, everything you can do to make the most of that time is going to be absolutely critical. That's why it's so important that you maintain your focus throughout your visit.

At the core of each of these tips is the idea that you want to do as much as possible to replicate what day to day life will be like in any community you eventually choose.

# CHAPTER 5
# PICK THE RIGHT REALTOR®

Once you've narrowed your ideal list of places down to 2-3 locations, that is a good time to start thinking about looking for an agent to help you with the "community" and "home" parts of the Pick the Right Place process.

If you took the initiative to purchase and read this book, you know better than to simply trust that the first real estate agent who crosses your path will be able to adequately handle the complex details of your real estate purchase.

Unfortunately, this is not the case for many people.

According to the National Association of REALTORS®, 70 percent of people complete a real estate transaction with the first agent they made contact with.

In order to find the very best real estate agent for you, first ask friends or family who have moved to the area you are considering for referrals. If you don't have anyone to contact in the area you are considering, try doing an internet search, such as "Orlando real estate agent," and investigate the websites of several agents that come up.

Also, try contacting the chamber of commerce for the city you plan to move to and see if they have any recommendations. It is a good idea to contact at least a few agents in the early stages to get a feel for what to expect down the road.

Be open and forthright with them if you have used the services of another agent before contacting them, so that there are no surprises for anyone later.

Ask the agents questions about their qualifications, years of experience in their market, and whether they have helped other people, particularly boomers like you, relocate to their area. They should be able to offer you written testimonials from satisfied clients.

Also, since you will be new to the area, make sure the real estate agent has a strong network of local service providers such as attorneys, home inspectors, and lenders to recommend to you.

### Need Help Finding an Agent?

I've been at this a long time and as you might imagine I've built relationships with agents in most of the major retirement hot spots.

If you'd like my help finding an agent in the area you are interested in, visit:

**https://www.PicktheRightPlace.com/agent**

# CHAPTER 6
# TYPES OF COMMUNITIES

There are several kinds of communities that you may come across in your search, and here I've detailed a few of the more popular types. Keep in mind that its entirely possible to come across communities that are combinations of these, for example, a gated 55+ maintenance-free community.

**Country Club Communities**

Most places have several golf course communities, also referred to as Country club communities. Courses can range rom fairly modest to extremely upscale.

Many communities have more than one golf course. Most have at least one clubhouse with such amenities as a fitness center, practice facilities, pro shop, restaurants and bars, banquet facilities, even full service spas, so that you can enjoy a massage after that tough round of golf.

Some golf courses are private, meaning you must be a

member or the guest of a member to play there. Membership rates vary among country clubs depending on the location and caliber of the course.

Keep in mind that most private courses have a food and beverage minimum, meaning that you have to spend at least "x" amount of dollars in their restaurants and bars within a designated period of time. Thankfully, sometimes purchases in the pro shop can be applied towards meeting your food and beverage minimum.

If you lose as many golf balls as I do, you should have no problem reaching your food and beverage minimum!

Many country club communities have equity member-ships, which pass from one party to another through the sale of real estate in that community. If this is the case with the home you intend to purchase, be sure that the real estate contract includes the right to the membership. Your real estate agent can help you with this.

Some communities have both a private course and a public course. You can own a home in a community such as this, not be a member and instead choose to play the public course exclusively. Surely, though, if your budget allows you will probably want to be a member of the private course to give your golf game some variety.

Country club communities with a golf course that is always open to the public are also an option. Be aware, however, that public courses tend to be more crowded than private courses, although this can depend on the time of year, the level of the course, and the price you have to pay to play. Some new communities allow the public to use their golf courses until there are enough residents and consequently enough members in the community. This is both good common sense and sound economics.

If you do not play golf, you may want to think twice about buying a home in a golf course community. Many people who do not play golf resent the fact that they are sometimes required to help fund its operations through their homeowners' association dues. Whether or not this occurs depends on how the homeowners' association and club budgets are set up, so you might want to look into that before you buy.

### Active Adult / 55-Plus communities

55-plus communities are communities where the majority of the homeowners are over the age of 55. In Florida for instance, for a community to qualify for the 55-plus designation and to be marketed as such, at least 80 percent of the units have to be occupied by at least one person over 55.

A common misconception is that everyone must be over 55 but that simply isn't true. On the other hand, this does not mean that someone under 55 must be allowed to purchase a home. A community -- through its deed restrictions -- can legally deny someone the ability to purchase a home if they are not yet 55 years old.

### Maintenance-Free Lifestyle Communities

If cutting grass, landscaping, painting, pressure washing, and general upkeep of the exterior of your home are appealing to you, skip to the next section.

Still with me?

Okay then, a maintenance-free community might be for

you. While some maintenance-free communities are designated 55 and better, most are not.

Maintenance-free communities are those in which you pay a monthly, quarterly, or yearly fee (sorry, the "free" in "maintenance-free" doesn't refer to the cost) to a homeowners' association or resident association, and in return, the association contracts with outside vendors to take care of certain maintenance and upkeep. Some homeowners' associations fees just include the cutting of your grass and leave the homeowner to take care of other items or contract with vendors directly to have them done. Others include complete landscaping such as shrub trimming, mulching, fertilizing and spraying of the yards, painting, and pressure washing.

Most maintenance-free communities are highly "amenticised", with clubhouses, swimming pools, billiard and card tables, craft rooms, fitness centers, and activity directors. The idea is that you fill your time doing the things you enjoy, while leaving the work to someone else.

**Manufactured Home Communities**

Most people entertaining the purchase of a manufactured home will be considering manufactured home communities that offer a full array of amenities like golf, tennis, swimming pools, clubhouses, and restaurants and bars.

It's not just the home, it's the lifestyle that people are after, and many developers have realized this and are offering it to the manufactured home buyer.

However, in many (though not all) manufactured home communities, you do not own the land your home sits on, the developer does.

One of the main factors in a home's ability to appreciate is its location and land value, something that in this arrangement you have almost no stake in. This is often times a thorn in the side of residents, but it is what it is. If you really want to live there, it's simply something you'll have to deal with.

Also, the developer will pay the taxes and provide the services outlined in the developer agreement such as grounds maintenance, lawn care, security, and the like, and in turn will charge you a fee, commonly referred to as "lot rent." This is a source of revenue for the developer. The developer is providing you certain services, and you are paying him for providing them. Likewise, when he has an increase in costs or taxes, these increases will be passed on to the homeowners.

One of the best ways to find out more about what owning and living in a manufactured home community might be like is to talk with people who live in one.

If you are curious, when visiting an area spend some time driving around a manufactured home community and talk with some residents if possible. Most will be glad to share their experiences with you, whether they are good or bad.

# CHAPTER 7
# DIFFERENT TYPES OF GATED COMMUNITIES

One of the most requested features among those searching for new home communities is that they be gated. There are various types of gated communities, some more secure than others. In this chapter, we'll look at the different types of gated communities you may come across in your search, as well as information about each type that will help you pick the one that's right for you.

All right, the first type of gated community is those with automatic gates. Due to their cost-effectiveness, automatic gates are probably the most common form of gated community you will come across in your search. How they work is, there will either be a gate arm that raises and lowers or a bigger metal or aluminum gate that swings open. You'll typically have a button on your garage door remote programmed to open the gate.

Gates like this will also have a call box so that visitors, mail carriers, and service people can get into the community when needed. Each resident will have their name programmed into the call box. When a visitor gets to the gate, they'll find your name in the list and it will ring to your house. You'll press a designated combination of keys on your phone to grant them access, and the gate will open for them. You'll also be given your own passcode, usually a four digit number, so that you can get in the gate if you find yourself without your opener, and nobody home to buzz you in.

A major security drawback with this kind of gated community is that, quite often, residents will give out their four digit security code to their visitors and service people. As soon as these codes pass from residents to non-residents, security is compromised. Some communities with automatic gates also have video cameras installed at the entry and exit points, which can be helpful for solving crimes after the fact, but not so good when it comes to prevention.

The next step up is a guard gated community. These communities typically have a guard shack where the gate attendant will be located. Some communities hire professionals for this role, while other communities depend on residents taking turns staffing the gate. So that residents are not delayed entering their own community, there will usually be two lanes, one for residents and one for non-residents. Residents will typically have a sticker in the corner of their windshield so the gate attendant knows to let them pass.

The guards definitely act as a deterrent and keep the

"looky-loos" out of the community. These communities are probably more secure than those with automatic gates, but still not as secure as the kind we'll discuss next. It's also important to note that some guard gated communities only staff the gates during the day, and revert to the automatic gate system at night. If 24 hour security is important to you, make sure you ask before you buy into a community like this what the gate staffing situation is.

The final kind of gated community we'll talk about is guard-gated communities with roving patrols. As far as gated communities go, this is about as secure as they get. Now, in addition to the guarded entry gate we already discussed, communities like these add roving patrols to the mix. The roving patrols perform several valuable functions. The most obvious one is that they drive around the community looking for anything suspicious or out of place.

In many communities with roving patrols, residents can alert the security staff if they'll be leaving for long stretches at a time, and the security staff will perform periodic house checks; making sure all the doors are locked, windows are closed, and so on. Last but not least, the roving patrols can assist residents with things like flat tires or help visitors find where they're going in the community.

With all that said, why don't all communities go with guards and roving patrols? The main reason most communities forgo guards and roving patrols is costs. It's very expensive to hire companies with trained professionals to staff the gates. When you add roving patrols to the mix, you have not only the additional manpower, but the cost of gas and vehicle maintenance to contend with.

In the early days of a community when very few residents have moved in, developers will be the ones footing the bill for all this, and many simply just don't want to do that. In some of the communities you'll look at, the developer will build a guard shack and tell prospective buyers that once there are enough residents, they, the residents can decide if they want to foot the bill to have it staffed. This always sounds like a reasonable explanation, but I can tell you that the amount of communities I've seen decide to add guards after the fact is pretty small. Residents get used to paying whatever it is they're paying, and when they see how much it's going to cost for guards, they balk and they don't do it.

If this level of security with guard gated with roving patrols is important to you, there's a lot of benefit in choosing a well established community where this type of security is already in place, and funded by thousands of residents, rather than a few hundred. Essentially, the more households the costs are spread across, the less each individual has to pay. Now, there is now perfect solution here. From personal experience, I can tell you that no matter which kind of gated community you choose, there's still a chance crime will occur.

For many years, I lived in a gated community with roving patrols, and one time my car was stolen right out of my garage! With a quick call to the front gate, the entry and exit gates were immediately shut down, and the thief was not able to leave the community. They had to ditch my car and take off on foot.

They got away, but on the bright side, at least I got my car back. Now, had I lived in a community that wasn't gated or just had an automatic gate, I may never have seen that car again. As you search for the perfect community, you'll have to decide for yourself which kind of gated community is best for you.

# CHAPTER 8
## COMMUNITY PREFERENCES

D ecide which of the following community preferences are most important to you in the list below. If it helps you figure out what's most/least important, rate each item on a scale of 0-10, with 0 being "Highly Undesirable" and 10 being "Highly Desirable".

Do you want to live in a community with a strict homeowners association?

Do you want to live in a community with a relaxed homeowners association?

Do you want to live in a community with no homeowners association?

Do you want to live in a community with lawn/landscaping maintenance included?

Do you want to live in a community where each home-owner takes care of their own lawn/ landscaping?

Do you want to live in a community that allows Boats/RV parking?

Do you want to live in a community that allows fences?

Do you want to live in a community close to shopping and restaurants?

Do you want to live in a more secluded community?

Do you want to live in a community with lots of amenities (pools, clubhouses, etc.)?

Do you want to live in a community with few amenities?

Do you want to live in a golf community?

Do you want to live in a community without a golf course?

Do you want to live in an age-restricted community?

Do you want to live in a community with people of all ages?

Do you want to live in a gated community?

Are there any other Community Preferences that come to mind for you?

Congratulations! After completing this exercise, you'll have developed some rough ideas of what your ideal community might look like.

Sharing the results of this exercise with your real estate

agent after you have completed it can help them narrow down the list of communities they show you, saving everyone a lot of time and effort.

# CHAPTER 9
# HOMEOWNERS ASSOCIATIONS

The general idea behind a homeowners' association (HOA) is that you have a group of people elected by the residents who make up the board directing the homeowners association.

The main duties are to 1) represent the best interests of the residents of the community especially in the capacity of protecting home values through the implementation and enforcement of rules, known as covenants and restrictions and 2) to assess and collect homeowners' fees to help pay for the upkeep of common areas of the community as well as any other areas provided for in the covenants and deed recordings.

**Fees and Dues**

Homeowners' association dues vary widely depending on the amount of amenities that are provided to the homeowners. Some just cover the maintenance of the common areas including medians, right of ways, lakes, and ponds.

Other dues can cover things such as upkeep of the streets (if they are private streets), and streetlights. Some communities negotiate for a group rate on cable TV or Internet access with service providers.

You may be charged fees for those services monthly, quarterly, or yearly. Failure to pay your homeowner's dues can result in the association placing a lien on your property and eventually foreclosing if you get far enough behind on your payments.

As a prospective purchaser in a community, you are entitled to and encouraged to review the budget. When deciding whether a homeowners' association's dues are a good deal or not, add up what you think it would cost you to obtain the services provided on your own.

Don't forget the aggravation the association saves you by not having to deal with finding and scheduling the services and vendors yourself.

If you are buying a home in a new subdivision where homes are still under construction, odds are that the developer still controls the homeowners' association. Until control of the HOA is given to the resident owners, called turnover, which the state of Florida requires to occur when 90% of the units in a community have sold and closed, the developer is still responsible for maintaining the public aspects of the community (streets, common areas, etc.) and carrying out the duties of creating a budget for the Association and setting HOA dues accordingly.

Oftentimes the developer will over-subsidize the budget, in order to keep the initial HOA fees low, in an effort to attract more buyers. But when turnover occurs, and the developer is no longer subsidizing the budget, homeowners can be hit with a sharp increase in their HOA dues. Before purchasing in a community where the developer controls the HOA, make sure that you carefully review the budget to make sure everyone is paying their fair share, or if that is not the case, try to reasonably figure out what your dues might be when control of the development turns over.

**Common Rules and Regulations**

Another aspect of communities with homeowners' associations is that most involve rules and regulations, or covenants and restrictions (C and Rs) also referred to as covenants, conditions, and restrictions (C, C and Rs). Be sure to ask for a copy before you sign any purchase agreement, and make sure that the agreement is contingent on (depends upon) your understanding and approval of the covenants and restrictions and rules and regulations.

Some common rules and regulations that may be included in the documents are rules regarding:

**Fences**

Some communities have restrictions on what type of fence you may have, the material it can be made of, how high it can be, or if any fences are allowed at all. If a community you are considering does not allow fences at all, and you have pets that require being fenced in, you might have to consider an invisible fence.

**Playground or sports equipment**

Basketball hoops are not allowed in more and more communities, while some allow portable basketball hoops as long as they are stored in the garage when not in use. Swing sets and slides are also commonly not allowed because of how they can deteriorate in appearance, and in maintenance-free communities where lawn care is included they are a hindrance to the easy cutting of your lawn.

### Parking

Overnight or long-term street parking are often not allowed. This is as much a fire and police safety issue as it is an aesthetic issue. Boats and trailers are usually not allowed to be stored outside, so you must find room in your garage or park them offsite.

### Changes to the exterior of your home

Most homeowners' associations require that an architectural or design review committee approve any changes you wish to make to the exterior of your home. This includes things such as adding a screened-in patio, swimming pool, or painting your home a different color. Even changes to your landscaping must sometimes be approved.

There is usually a form they have you fill out on which you must describe in detail any changes you plan to make, including a list of materials to be used, who will do the work, and so on. You are also typically required to submit any drawings or plans that show how the change will look when complete. This is to keep everything in the neighborhood looking nice and congruent.

### Pets

Some communities have restrictions on the number of

pets you may have in a home, as well as the size. These are typically implemented to reduce the number of potentially aggressive dogs such as pit bulls, and are most common in condominiums or townhouses due to the close proximity of your neighbors. Also, most communities and municipalities now have rules requiring you to pick up after your pets. Be mindful of these rules and laws, especially if the area you are moving from had no such ordinances, as you can be heavily fined for ignoring them.

### Protection of home values

It can sound like a pain to have to pay these fees and abide by these restrictions especially if you are coming from a community that doesn't have any fees or restrictions. But all these fees and rules, as inconvenient as they may sometimes seem, do serve the important purpose of protecting your home values. If you are going to pay a quarter of a million dollars or more for your new home, you want to know that someone is looking out for you and your investment. Ask any reputable real estate agent or property appraiser and they will tell you that communities governed by homeowners' associations have the best track record of preserving and increasing home values.

### Deciding if an HOA is for you

So, based on the above information, do you think a community with a homeowners' association is for you? If you're at all like me, the answer is a resounding yes. I like knowing that my best interests are being looked after and my home value is being protected. You basically just have to weigh out the pros and cons of living in such a structured environment. While it's not for everybody, I think that most people, especially boomers such as you will ultimately choose to live in and be happy in communities with a homeowners' association. I think it's best for your lifestyle and the future value of your property.

**Condo Association Fees**

As an owner of a condominium you will be responsible for paying condo fees. Before buying a condo, make sure these fees have been explained to you in writing. You should also ask to see the budget. When buying a resale condo in Florida you have a three-day "cooling off" period (7 days for new condo construction) during which you may ask to cancel your contract. This is so that potential condo buyers have ample opportunity to examine and understand the condo fees, rules, and budget. Remember though that this only applies to condos, the same "cooling off" period does not apply to any other type of property.

The condo fees are collected to pay for things like maintenance of the exterior of the condo, including insurance on the building, maintenance of the common areas, such as the grounds, swimming pool, and other amenities. Quite frequently in a condo the condo fee includes water, sewer, and garbage service. This is often more convenient for you: almost no one complains about having a few less checks to write.

**Special Assessments**

Eventually, if you live in a condo or homeowners' association long enough, you may fall prey to what is called a special assessment. A special assessment is sometimes a necessary evil, and is used to pay for items such as a new roof or unexpected repairs beyond ordinary maintenance. Your association's budget should have a reserve set aside for unexpected events, but sometimes if there is not enough money to pay for what needs to be done, unit owners will be assessed. If you are on a shoestring budget or have a fixed income with little reserves, you may want to rethink a condo because just one special assessment can put you in the red.

Also note that failure to pay any of your condo fees or special assessments can result in the condo association placing a lien on your property, which can eventually lead to foreclosure.

# CHAPTER 10
# WHAT YOU DON'T WANT IN A COMMUNITY

When you begin looking through some of the options for active adult communities that might interest you, you might be amazed to find out exactly how many of them there are out there.

As you proceed with your search for the perfect community, you will naturally gravitate towards focusing on your must haves for a community. Concerning yourself with what types of benefits a particular community has is a great place to start, but don't forget that you also want to be on the lookout for things that you do not want in a retirement community.

In order to help you out on that front, I've put together a list of things that you definitely want to avoid in a retirement community.

The first thing is overbuilt communities. What's the easiest way to tell if a community has been overbuilt and is grown too big for its infrastructure? Traffic. As you were driving around the community, take note of the traffic levels, particularly at busy intersections.

Waiting in traffic might not bother you too much while you're in the excited community shopping phase of your relocation. But imagine dealing with the traffic you encounter on a daily basis.

Even if a community isn't overbuilt just yet, you should be checking on their plans for expansion to make sure that it won't become overbuilt after you already committed to living there.

One of the problems that tends to go hand-in-hand with overbuilt communities is crowded communities. When many active adult communities expand and grow, increasing the capacities of their amenities is sometimes last on the to-do list.

In those situations, you're going to have a hard time getting a chair at the pool or a treadmill at the fitness center or a tee time at the golf course. And that doesn't sound like anyone's version of the ideal retirement. Once again, it will pay serious dividends for you to ask about the community's plan for expansion so that you know what you're getting into before you commit.

As you continue shopping for the perfect community, you will likely notice that just about every community boasts a state-of-the-art fitness center as one of their featured amenities.

Unfortunately, many communities have very different opinions on what exactly state-of-the-art means.

Take a good look at all the amenities as you tour a potential community. Make sure that they appear to be recently updated and kept in good shape. If a community has not kept up with their amenities before you move there, they likely won't bother to do so after you move there either.

Some of the communities you consider will tempt to lure you in with first-class amenities and then charge you thousands more for a house compared to what it would cost in another community.

There's nothing wrong with paying more for homes in a nicer community as long as you are making a conscious decision to do so and not being lured into paying more than you would for a home of the exact same quality and the same features somewhere else.

Another thing that you don't want to overpay for is amenities that you won't use. Some of the more elaborate communities have amazing amenities, but if you aren't going to make use of them, you might be throwing money away. Be honest with yourself about what amenities you will actually use and which ones you probably won't ever get around to using.

Depending on your personality and energy level, you also want to keep an eye out for communities that might just be a bit too active for your tastes, especially if you're looking at a house that is close to an activities center. There's nothing wrong with wanting to spend your retirement quietly sitting outside after a calm round golf, but that isn't the type of vibe you're going to find everywhere so be aware of what you're getting into.

On the other hand, you don't want a community that is too calm for your taste either. If no one is ever doing anything then your retirement years are doomed to be pretty boring. Regardless of how active you choose to be during your retirement, there's a community out there that is a perfect fit for that lifestyle so don't settle for anything less!

Last but not least, let's talk about restrictions.

Restrictions are great when they are limited to a healthy extent. You probably don't want your neighbor to paint their house neon green and with the restrictions that are in place in most communities that likely won't happen.

But one of the easiest ways to ruin your experience in any community is to be aggravated by an overly strict set of rules you must abide by. Make sure you talk with some current residents about what they think of the community restrictions before you commit to a particular community.

Each of these things to avoid in a retirement community might seem obvious while you're sitting at home thinking about your plans to move, but be careful!

As you visit different communities, you'll be tempted to ignore some of the obvious signs that a community might not be the right fit for you. Make sure you go in with your eyes and ears wide open before you take the leap.

# CHAPTER 11

# THINGS TO CONSIDER BEFORE DECIDING ON A COMMUNITY

O nce you decide on your short list for places to retire, you're going to want to zoom in on the places and communities that will best fit with your lifestyle expectations. In this chapter we'll cover six critical things you will absolutely want to consider before you decide on moving forward with any one particular community.

Location is the name of the game in the real estate world as everybody knows. You'll want to assess the location of any community you're considering with respect to nearby towns and cities. Your dream retirement community could turn into a nightmare pretty quickly if you have to drive for over an hour every time you need groceries.

One of the most common mistakes that people make in searching for a retirement community is trying to determine whether lifestyle would fit into a particular community. Instead you should be asking if the community promotes the type of lifestyle you're looking for. There are large and small communities out there. Some are very active. Some are more on the quiet side. Whichever type of lifestyle fits your goals is where you should be looking to retire.

Just about every community these days has some pretty impressive amenities but another thing to consider is how well the amenities of a particular community fit with your lifestyle. Having a beautiful 18-hole golf course won't be all that helpful if you aren't a golfer. On the other hand, if you a big time golfer that same course might not be enough. You should focus on evaluating the amenities that you'll actually be using and how well they fit your vision of retirement.

You also don't want to find the perfect community only to realize that the homes there are all either too big or too small for what you're looking for. Now most communities will have a wide range of sizes but it pays to understand exactly how much space you're going to need, how much you can afford and where you're willing to be flexible on both accounts.

This one's pretty simple. If you don't like your potential neighbors after meeting them for just a few minutes, how are you going to feel after living next to them for 10 years? Be very careful to choose a location where the general vibe of the people in the community is positive and fits with your lifestyle goals.

Last but not least is travel time. Some might consider this a part of analyzing location but it is so important that it gets its own section. If you're going to be traveling back home, inviting friends and family to come visit you, or planning to vacation regularly, you're going to want to have easy access to interstates and airports. Figure out exactly how long it will take you to travel to wherever you might be going and whether that's an acceptable distance to you and the people who might be coming to visit you.

Again, these may seem like obvious things to consider but if you happen to commit to a home where one of them doesn't fit your lifestyle, you run the costly risk of having to reverse your decision down the road.

# CHAPTER 12
## BEST PLACES FOR COMMUNITY RESEARCH

The internet is both a blessing and a curse, especially as it relates to researching places to retire. For instance, if you go to Google and type in the phrase "Florida Retirement Communities" you'll get back about 80,700,000 results, of which only a handful will likely prove valuable to you. In this chapter I'm going to help you get on the right track as far as research is concerned, and point you to the handful of sites and resources that I believe will prove most helpful to you.

All right, so of that 80 million plus websites that Google tells you might be a good place to start I feel like there's a handful of them that I should tell you about right off the bat, which will provide the highest return on your time spent here.

I might be biased, but if you are focused solely on Florida, I recommend you start with my website at:

FloridaForBoomers.com

There you can read our community reviews and request brochures from a number of different communities without having to leave our site.

But one thing that differentiates my site from some of the others I'll mention below is that we put a little more emphasis on what it's like to live in Florida, and in each area. I cover things like cost of living, taxes, places to see, things to do, and so on.

If you are looking for communities outside of Florida, one site you should check out is 55Places.com. This website covers more than 2,000 communities across the country, and what I like most about it, and what I think you'll benefit most from is that they give really detailed information about each community.

Ideal-Living.com is another website you should check out. What really makes them different are their retirement expos they hold in different locations. These are usually in the Northeast and Midwest during the winter, because why not go and get in front of people where and when they're bound to be the coldest and growing tired of shoveling snow.

At these expos they have people from communities all over the country come in and set up booths, and it basically gives you the opportunity to go around, check out the places that look most interesting to you, and get more information, or maybe even set up a trip to go visit. They also have people come in and give talks at these expos on different retirement topics.

So if you live near where they're having one of these shows, definitely go check one out. I've worked a number of these shows over the years and they're good fun.

# CHAPTER 13

# QUESTIONS TO ASK YOUR FUTURE NEIGHBORS

W hen you visit communities to figure out which one you want to live in, one of the most important things you could do for yourself is talk to as many people who actually live there as possible.

Maybe you're taking advantage of one of the Stay and Play opportunities that many communities offer, in which case you'll probably have a few days to meet several residents and learn what they like and don't like about the community.

But even if you're just visiting for the day and getting the official sales presentation, you need to find a way to break free from the salespeople and strike up a conversation with as many residents as you can.

In great communities, salespeople realize their residents are the BEST salespeople, and they'll have no hesitation about you talking to the residents. Some communities even set you up with a resident ambassador to facilitate this process.

If you're ever in a community though and get the sense they don't want you to talk to other residents, that could be a bad sign.

Here's what you should be asking.

**1. Where are they from?**

Finding common ground quickly is important if you truly want them to open up to you.

Asking people where they're from can help you find that common ground. Maybe you're not from the same place as they are, but maybe you know someone from there or you've visited in the past.

Either way, this is a great place to start and you can also get some good information about what it was like adjusting to life here.

**2. How long have they lived here?**

With this question you're trying to figure out just how much experience they possibly have to share with you.

If they're a fairly new resident, that can be a good thing. Everything you're about to go through will be fresh in their mind and you can get a lot of helpful hints about things like home selection, lot selection and so on from people like this.

If they've lived in the community a few years or longer, this can be a good thing too. First, you know they liked it enough to stay. It's good to hear they didn't move in and hate it so much that they immediately started looking for another community.

Plus, they'll have a better understanding of the inner

workings of the community that they'll hopefully feel free to share with you.

**3.What model did you buy?**

For whatever reason, people tend to be super-proud of whichever floorplan they chose. Even if it's not the size or style you're thinking about buying, hear them out. You never know what great insights might escape their lips.

Related to this you can ask what they building process was like, what changes they would have made to the home (if any) in hindsight.

All of this can help you immensely no matter what type of home you buy or where you buy it.

**4.Where in the community did they buy?**

If it's a small community, this doesn't matter as much. But if it's a big sprawling master-planned community, it's a very important question.

Different neighborhoods within the community can have drastically different vibes, and pluses and minuses.

Try to get to the root of why they chose to purchase where they did.

**5. Do they live in the community full-time?**

If you're planning to snowbird for a few years at first this is a great way to figure out who your fellow snowbirds are and what it's like to lock and leave your home for months at a time.

What types of services (security, house check, mainte-nance, etc.) do they employ while they're gone to keep an eye on their home and how do they like them?

If they live there full-time, try to get a sense of what the different times if year are like in the community. Are certain times more crowded or less crowded than others, and what is that like?

**6.Do they plan to stay here forever?**

Nobody can predict the future, but most people have some sense of whether this will be their forever home or if they see themselves outgrowing the community in some way.

Maybe they like their home but they heard about the future golf course community being built a few miles away and they're interested in checking that out.

Either way, this question can elicit some very helpful information.

**7. What do they think about other communities in the area?**

If their response is to belittle all the other communities around, however rude it may seem, it's not necessarily a bad thing. Maybe they're just passionate about the community they chose and very happy with their choice.

(Sidenote: A salesperson should NEVER do this. If they do, it should raise red flags! It's o.k. for them to point out the ways in which their community might be better, but they should never say something like, "Oh, that community is terrible ... you don't want to look there.")

Back to the residents, see if they know anyone who lives in the other communities you might be considering. Maybe they've met these other people through church, civic, or social groups. The more leads you get for people to talk to and learn from, the better.

**Don't Be Shy!**

Don't be shy about any of this. The residents you're going to meet were in your shoes one day not too long ago, and they'll remember and empathize with what you're going through and the decisions you're grappling with.

In almost 100% of cases, you'll find that the residents you try to talk to will be more than happy to give you at least a few minutes of their time and tell you what you want to know.

Some of them will be so excited to talk to someone new you might not be able to get them to shut up once you've heard enough.

That's o.k. Good or bad, let them get everything off their chest. You never know what they might say, positive or negative, that might help in this important decision.

# CHAPTER 14
## TYPES OF HOMES

When considering a home purchase, one of the first decisions you should make is whether to have a home built, or buy a resale (previously occupied) home. Your decision will depend on several factors including how quickly you need a home, your personal taste, and other factors. Here are some pros and cons of both.

**Benefits of Building a New Home**

One of the first benefits of building new versus buying a resale is that when you choose to build your new home from scratch, you get to build it the way you want it. You'll have the option to choose the ideal floor plan you want, and you will also be able to choose the materials and color schemes that fit your personality and tastes.

Another big selling point for new home construction is that you'll have the ability to customize many aspects of your home. Adding features like a pot filler above the stove, or a particular type of recessed lighting in a certain spot, are easy to integrate when they're added before the walls go up.

Through your process of looking at communities and comparing home builders, you'll find that some are happy to accommodate most reasonable customization requests for a fee of course, but you'll also find some that aren't willing to change their floor plans or let you customize your new home at all. There's very little way to tell from the outset which camp a builder falls into until you have a conversation with their sales team. So be sure to make it one of the first things you ask about when looking at a community.

Continuing on, another benefit to buying new is the new home warranty. Should anything go wrong with your new construction home in the first few years it will almost certainly be covered under your warranty. The same can't be said with a resale home, where what you see is often what you get, and you could be opening yourself up to tremendous risk if something goes wrong down the road. Now, don't get me wrong. You *can* buy warranties for resale homes. They're just typically not going to be as comprehensive as new home warranties.

The next benefit of buying or building new versus buying a resale that I'd like to cover, is energy efficiency. Whether you're concerned about protecting the environment or more interested in protecting your bank account from high energy costs, the modern green technologies that will likely be included in your new home will actually be able to do both. Your new home is sure to have energy efficient appliances, and it may also feature energy saving technologies in its roofing materials, windows and air conditioning systems, which can save you thousands of dollars in energy costs over time.

On a similar note, new homes will require less maintenance. Your home will already have a fresh coat of paint and a brand new roof, air conditioner, appliances and other components. So those types of maintenance projects and replacements will hopefully not be necessary until several years down the road. In some cases you'll also be able to choose and design your landscaping in a way that can help you save on maintenance there as well.

Now should you ever decide to sell, odds are you'll get higher resale value when you go to sell if your house is one of the newest homes in the community as opposed to if it's one of the older homes in the community. It makes sense, right? But it's not something most people consider when they're trying to decide between building new or buying a resale.

Last but not least, another advantage of purchasing a new home is the feeling of knowing that you're the only person who has ever lived there, and for some people that alone is worth a lot. You will never have to consider what might've happened in the home before you lived there. Everything will brand new and custom built just for you.

**Cons of Building a New Home**

One of the cons of building a new home is that you typically have to wait for the home to be built, unless the builder has the style of home you want in their inventory (commonly referred to as "spec" homes or "quick move-in" homes). If you are on a tight schedule, or you do not want to find a temporary place to live while your home is under construction, you might want to pass on building a new home.

Another important factor to consider is that building a new home can be an overwhelming and nerve-wracking process. Seeing little day-to-day progress can be exasperating and many people feel the urge to micromanage the builder when there is usually no need to do that. If you are predisposed to being a micromanager, skip the headaches and buy a home that's already built.

**Benefits of Buying a Resale Home**

Undoubtedly, some of you might have your heart set on building or buying a brand new home in retirement, and that's fine. So far I've built two houses in my lifetime, and I totally understand that desire. It's probably something you've been dreaming about for a long time. But even if that's the case, it will serve you well to know about some of the advantages of buying or least considering a resale.

The first advantage of buying a resale versus buying or building a new home is price. You'll typically find that resales tend to be priced just a bit lower than the newly built homes in the community. It makes sense, right? They probably should be. They've got a few more miles on them so to speak and they're a couple of years into their warranties. Plus, homes built just a few years ago might not have some of the newer features the builder might be including now versus when the home was first built.

I can remember back in my new home sales days, when we'd have one of the residents come into the model home to get an updated brochure and list of prices under the guise of, they have a friend back home who's interested and they want to send them the latest info. Then a couple weeks later you see that same resident has a for sale sign in their yard. What they were doing was simply doing their homework and figuring out how they could price their home competitively in relation to the new homes.

Lower prices is definitely a reason to consider a resale. Along with that I might also add the ability to negotiate, which some builders, depending on the market, are just reluctant to do at all.

The second advantage of buying a resale is that new construction is a hassle. Having built a couple houses in my day, I can tell you that no matter where you're building it or who is building it, there are just going to be some hassles. Whether it's before, during, after or all three, there's going to be times when you wish you'd looked a little closer at some resales and not had to go through all these issues and stress. Sometimes it will be little things, like the wrong kind of tile gets installed accidentally or some other small detail goes awry.

Other times it will be bigger stuff, like the builder builds your house on the wrong lot, or flip the opposite way of how you thought it was going to be laid out. Don't laugh, I've seen both of those things actually happen, and they weren't pretty. Now typically all this stuff works out in the end, and after a while you forget about most of the little stuff. But if you want to avoid the pain altogether you might want to consider a resale.

Next up is location. Depending on the community this

could be a biggie. If you're building a new home, it's going to be located in whichever part of the community the builder happens to be building at that particular point in time. Most communities are built in different phases over the course of several months or several years. But lets say one of the items on your must-have list is a short walk to the clubhouse or amenity center. If all the houses in that part of the community have already been built you're going to be out of luck, unless you're willing to consider the possibility of a resale. So location is another good reason to keep an open mind to that possibility.

The final advantage of considering a resale I'd like to cover has to do with the option and features available in the homes you're looking at. Now this will vary from community to community and builder to builder, but as I've mentioned before, some builders are more lenient than others on letting buyers choose specific options and features. In communities where builders don't offer much flexibility, it's often like,

> "Glad to hear that's what you'd like Mr Buyer, but here's how we build them. Take it or leave it. You can always change stuff or add new stuff after you close."

Now building 1,000 different houses 1,000 different ways is tough for any builder to manage, so if they can build 1,000 houses 10 or 20 different ways, well that's just much easier for them. They know the houses are going to sell eventually, at least that's what they hope, so it's very much a business decision. In communities where changes and getting the options and features you want is more challenging, you might want to take a good hard look at some of the resales available.

In many of the cases you'll find that the owners of resales have gone ahead and added some of the options and upgrades you actually want. So rather than buying new and having to do all this stuff on your own after moving in, if you find the right resale it may already be done for you.

I could go on here but I think you get the point of what I'm trying to tell you. That's, don't short change yourself by neglecting resales altogether. There really are some worthwhile advantages available to those willing to keep an open mind in considering buying a resale rather than building a new home.

**Cons of Resale Homes**

With a resale home you are not able to choose your décor such as tile and carpet, cabinets and countertops, or make any customization or personalization until after the purchase and, even then, not without a remodeling budget. It is what it is. Someone else has chosen the colors and materials, and their tastes may differ from your own. Something else to consider is that, depending on the age and construction of the home, your insurance may cost more.

Additionally, if you want the protection of a home warranty, it must be purchased separately at your expense, unless the seller provides one. Also, don't forget you'll need a home inspection, which you can read more about in a later chapter.

**Should you Rent?**

Another possibility for you to consider is renting a home

for a year or two while you acclimate yourself to your new area. This can be helpful for anyone who isn't 100% sure they want to move to a certain place, or live in a certain neighborhood, or type of home. You can try it out, and when your lease is up, you can decide what to do from there.

Most experts agree that in most cases buying is better than renting. Not so much because of future appreciation that can take several years to realize, but for the tax benefits of owning, like deducting mortgage interest and real estate taxes.

Other problems with renting as opposed to buying include the difficulty of finding something that suits your tastes and housing needs. There's no such thing as a custom built rental. Plus, if you do find a place, since you don't own the home you'll be restricted in making any changes to its appearance.

All of that said though, in a situation where you are the least bit unsure of your decision, renting may be the answer. It would do you very little good to plunk down tons of money on a new home, only to decide you hate the area, and in six months or a year later pick up and find a new home in a new area.

### Single Family Homes

The most basic and most popular type of home is the single family home.

It's what most people think of when someone says "house". A standalone structure, a single family home sits on its own piece of land, be it the size of a credit card or several acres. Single family homes offer their owners the most sense of space.

Even if your neighbor's home is only five feet away, as will be the case in some communities, you still have a feeling of separation and distance from them. When standing in your living room, you really can't tell if the neighbor's house is five feet or 50 feet away.

Single-family homes typically offer the most flexibility when you wish to make changes, such as adding an addition, changing the exterior color, or putting in a pool.

If you buy a single-family home in a subdivision governed by a Homeowners' Association (HOA), you will not have as much flexibility with what you can do to your home.

The Architecture Review Board or ARB must typically approve most changes, especially those affecting the exterior appearance of the home. However the upside is that your neighbors will have to conform to the same standards when they wish to make changes. Be sure to read the HOA restrictions before purchasing to make sure they are rules you are willing to follow.

As an owner of a single family home, you will be responsible for the home's maintenance. You will be responsible for cutting the grass, trimming the shrubs and bushes, painting, pressure cleaning, and any other exterior maintenance as needed.

For the those who have better things to do than to spend their weekends doing yard work, however, the new trend in some communities is for single-family homes to be maintained on the outside, just like a townhouse or condo. These are called "maintenance-free communities" or "maintenance-free lifestyle communities." Just as in a townhouse or condo, the owner is assessed a fee to pay for certain services such as lawn care, periodic painting, and pressure washing.

### Condominiums

Condominiums, or condos, are an increasingly popular housing choice.

Condominiums are buildings comprised of several separate units. Theoretically, the price of the land that the condo is built on is spread across the units, with units on higher floors typically commanding higher prices and yielding better views.

For example, someone who wants to live on the ocean and may not be able to afford the several million-dollar price tags for a home may opt instead for a condo at a lower price. Even so, some condos run into the millions of dollars depending on location and features.

Condominiums are communities unto themselves. The beauty of condo living is that most of the upkeep of a regular single family home is eliminated. There is no lawn to cut, no shrubs to trim, and you won't ever be asked to paint the building in your spare time on the weekend. Amenities range from the bare bones with a swimming pool and fitness room, to total luxury with full-time concierge, doorman and valet, room service, spas, and restaurants.

I actually live in a condo on the ocean. There are things that I love about condo living and things that I don't like. Here are a few of each.

## WHAT I LIKE ABOUT CONDO LIVING

**(Almost) No Maintenance** – I love the fact that I don't own this task anymore. I think it annoys my wife because she can't make up some random outside chore just to get me out of the house anymore. Hahaha!

Obviously you're always going to have the minor inside stuff that comes up, but outside...that's somebody else's baby now.

We have a full-time maintenance man here at the condo. He's typically here from early in the morning until early afternoon. Whenever we notice things that need his attention, we just call or email the condo office and they get him right on it.

There is also a property manager on-site too. She keeps about the same hours as the maintenance guy. She's who we go to if we need to reserve the social room, need parking passes for guests, etc.

**I've Downsized My Life** – The condo we live in is actually bigger than our house by about 200 sq. ft., but it has one less room, which was my office. So, the rooms we have are bigger, but we have less places to hide all of our stuff. Before we moved, we really had to take inventory of the things that were essential/important to us and ditch the rest.

First to go were my books. I had a personal library of well over 300 books that I had accumulated over the years, and they were easy to store as my home office had built in bookshelves. But when we moved I boxed up 90% of them and donated them to the library. I probably never would have read them again, so I don't miss them.

The next thing to deal with was our wine collection. We don't have anything expensive or super fancy, just stuff we had bought at the few wine tastings we had attended or stuff people brought by during holidays and such.

We had really nice built in wine racks with plenty of room at our old house but not so here at the condo. So we drank a few bottles and gave some others away. We now have a small liquor cabinet, but nothing like the wine racks we had before.

Last but not least we lost closet space. At our old house we had his and her closets which worked out really nice. Now we share a closet and things are a little tighter. I got rid of a bunch of stuff I didn't wear and I feel better for it. I like it when my shirt color choices in the morning are between blue and blue. I'm a simple creature.

Even my wife got rid of a bunch of clothes she didn't wear anymore. Oh who am I kidding? We're still figuring the closet situation out!

All kidding aside, getting rid of things may not sound like a positive to some people, but for me, its really helped me realize that I feel better without having to find a place for so much stuff.

## WHAT I DON'T LIKE ABOUT OCEANFRONT CONDO LIVING

**You WILL hear the people above, beside, and below you -** Admittedly, I was naive and didn't think this would be a huge issue. The condo we live in was built in 2003 so I thought condo construction practices had evolved to the point of eliminating this pesky problem, but apparently not.

Most everyone gets along here at the condo, but I think everyone has moments where they wish the people in the units surrounding them would just be quiet.

Our biggest problem is that we tend to be late risers. Meanwhile the lady that lives above us is an early riser, and goes out onto her patio to watch the sunrise every single morning.

Because of where our bedroom is in relation to the patio, which is the same as her bedroom and patio we hear her get out of bed, use the bathroom, flush the toilet, open the sliding glass door, and adjust her chair to just the right sunrise viewing position. Then 20 minutes later, we pretty much hear the same, just in reverse.

If you're thinking about moving into a condo, and its not the penthouse, plan on having to deal with this issue.

**You can't pick your neighbors** – And I don't just mean your neighbors in the condo. Yes, we've got two or three real doozies here, but most everyone is pleasant enough.

What I really mean here though is that in a normal community, you can pretty much count on another house being right next to you. Heck, it might even look exactly like yours.

Here at our condo, just to the south of us we have a vacant lot and then an old hotel. The old hotel is currently shut down and undergoing renovations. I believe it is supposed to be a Hyatt Place when they are through, so that's not too bad.

But my biggest worry is what will become of the vacant lot. Now, I know the city, county, and local planning department will have a say in what can and will ever go there, but who knows? Dumb projects get approved all the time.

Nothing you can do about this though, and again, for us, it's not enough of a worry to make us want to leave, but it might be something you want to think about if you are considering a condo.

### Townhouses

Townhouses can be considered sort of a happy medium between a single family home and a condo. Townhouses are two-story structures that are similar to single family homes in that they sit on their own piece of land.

They are also like a condominium in that they are attached to one or more other homes. They commonly include either a one or two-car garage and also a front or back patio for lounging outside.

The outside of the home is typically taken care of for you, you don't have anyone living directly above you, and there is frequently a small piece of the yard for you to call your own in which you can plant annuals or a rose bush, etc. (often subject to community restrictions). These benefits account for the rise in popularity of townhouse living.

In most communities, townhouse owners are assessed for the maintenance of the common areas (parts of the community owned equally by the home owners), as well as any amenities provided such as swimming pools, tennis courts, and pavilions.

These assessments can occur monthly, bi-monthly, quarterly or yearly. Most likely these fees will not be figured into your mortgage, so you will have to make a separate payment when it is due. Again, you should review the budget and the association rules before you make a purchase.

**Manufactured Homes**

Close your eyes and step into a modern manufactured home. Now open them. Are you sure that you're really in a manufactured home? You see drywall, crown molding, tile, hardwood floors, a fireplace, decorative niches, and archways. Then look at the floorplan and layout, it seems that this can't be a manufactured home!

Manufactured homes have come a long way from the long and narrow tin cans on wheels of the 50s, 60s, and 70s and have evolved into a logical, economical, and safe choice for many would-be homeowners. Affordability is one of the main factors driving the increase in manufactured home ownership. Manufactured homes cost considerably less than their site-built counterparts, sometimes 25-50 percent less, in fact.

Money is one thing you say, but are they safe?

Today's manufactured homes are built in quality and environmentally controlled factories and adhere to current federal building codes.

This, combined with the fact that they are anchored to the foundation on which they sit, a process that is overseen by local building inspectors, means a safe and secure home that can withstand the elements. Manufactured home builders' websites are often filled with testimonials of how their homes have been able to withstand hurricane force winds just as well and sometimes better than some site-built homes.

Before you jump in though, some caveats to consider: Though they may be built to withstand winds over 100 mph and are up to federal codes, manufactured homes are still feared by many insurers. It can be tough to find insurance on your manufactured home at a reasonable rate.

Also, where I live here in Florida, when hurricanes threaten, especially near the coast, manufactured home communities are almost always under mandatory evacuation orders, even if site-built home communities surrounding them are only under voluntary evacuation orders.

That might be something to think about if you don't want to have to pick up and go every time the wind blows.

# CHAPTER 15
# DETERMINE YOUR HOUSING PREFERENCES

dentify the following features / amenities as they apply to your housing needs and wants.

**Home Type**

\_\_\_ Single-Family Home

\_\_\_ Townhouse

\_\_\_ Condo

\_\_\_ Single Story

\_\_\_ 2+ Story

\_\_\_ Concrete Block

\_\_\_ Wood Frame

\_\_\_ Maintenance-Free

\_\_\_ New Construction

\_\_\_ Resale

. . .

**Home Features**

Square footage: _____

Number of Bedrooms: ____

Number of Bathrooms: ____

____ 1-Car Garage

____ 2-Car Garage

____ 3+ Car Garage

____ Formal Living Room

____ Formal Dining Room

____ Great Room

____ Open Floor Plan

____ Office/Study or Den

____ Kitchen Island

____ Electric Appliances

____ Gas Appliances

____ Walk-In Closets

____ Fireplace

____ Screened Porch

____ Swimming Pool

**Price Range:** _____ to _____

**List Any Additional Housing Preferences Below:**

# CHAPTER 16
# NEGOTIATING WITH HOME BUILDERS

Your ability to negotiate with new home builders is going to depend primarily on whether the area you're buying a home in is in a seller's market, or a buyer's market.

In a buyer's market, of course, anything goes, and your chances of negotiating a great deal with a builder are greatly increased. But in a seller's market, it can be a little tougher to get a great deal, but that doesn't mean you can't get one or that you shouldn't ask.

I've personally experienced both an extreme buyer's market, and an extreme seller's market while working in new home sales, so I can provide some real-world in- sight as to what you might encounter in both types of markets.

Back in 2003 and 2004 when I was selling new homes here in Florida, it was definitely a seller's market. In both 2003 and 2004 we sold more than 100 homes a year, which for a community our size, was simply incredible. We had three sales people, and four or five model homes lined up in a row for people to walk through and see the different types of homes we built.

It really got to the point where some days we would be so busy that we would simply say to new people walking in, "Hi, welcome. Thanks for coming by. I'd really love to spend more time with you, but I have two other couples waiting for me in my office to write contracts. These are our models. Please take a look and let me know afterwards if you have any questions."

Not the greatest sales experience or interaction from the buyer's perspective, but it was just the reality of the market back then. Now, in those days, if you wanted to build a new home and negotiate on price, I didn't even have to call my sales manager. The answer was simply, "No, we don't negotiate the prices of our homes." In a seller's market, you're going to hear that over and over most places you go. "If you don't buy this house, I'm pretty confident one of the next 10 people to walk through that door will buy it and pay full price." But that doesn't mean people didn't get good deals back then.

One opportunity that might be available, even in a seller's market, are spec homes. Because the market was so hot, it wasn't likely that we had finished spec homes sitting around unsold, but I remember the few times we did. People got a great deal on those, despite the market conditions.

Now, typically those homes sat around and didn't sell for one or more reasons, like they were on a less desirable lot, maybe the decorator had a few too many glasses of Merlot when she picked out the interior color scheme, whatever the reason. But for people who could see past some of those issues in order to get what they considered a good deal, these homes presented a great opportunity.

Keep in mind, no matter what community you go into or what kind of market it is, a builder does not like to be sitting with completed spec homes. When a home is completed and has a certificate of occupancy, the builder is paying on that home just like a homeowner would.

That means not only the mortgage interest, but the taxes, insurance, HOA fees, plus the power bill, the water bill. They've got to pay somebody to cut the grass, they've got to pay somebody to keep it clean so it's presentable to perspective buyers. Bottom line: it all adds up.

Now, multiply that by three, four, or half a dozen completed spec homes sitting empty, and you can understand the urgency on the builder's part for getting a deal done. Each month that they have to carry that home in inventory is just eating away at their profit on that house. If you visit a community one month and come back a month later and the same finished home is still available, you know you've got some bargaining room.

Now, let's say that it's still a seller's market, but the builder has no completed specs sitting around. Then what do you do? First off, it never hurts to come right out and ask for a discount. They might not say yes, but at least you took a shot and they now know you're interested.

But even if they say no to your request for a discount right off the bat, you shouldn't stop there. See, money is not the only thing you can negotiate. You could say, "Hey, I'll pay your asking price, but I'd really prefer some stainless steel appliances instead of the white ones you have going in that house there." That's negotiating around options and upgrades, and builders take home a huge margin on most of their upgrades, so you could potentially have some negotiating room on those.

Next, is lot premiums. Now, lot premiums are the extra bit of money builders charge for what they determine to be the prime lots in the community. It could be that they back up to a pond, or a golf course, or a nature area, or maybe it's just a bigger corner lot. Now, when the builder bought the land from the community, they probably bought it all for one package price.

As long as they're selling you a house lot package, meaning the price includes the house and the lot, then the price they paid for the land is recovered in the base price of the home you're considering buying. Then, these lot premiums are 100% profit for the builder. Again, this is another area where it doesn't hurt to ask them to shave a few grand off.

Another thing you can sometimes negotiate for, even in a seller's market, is time, and sometimes time is worth more than money. Let's say you find your dream community and your dream home, and you know you need to lock it up before somebody else comes along and steals it out from under you.

But let's say it's going to take the builder six months to

build your home, but you know that back home it's taking an average 10 to 12 months for houses to sell. You want a little extra time to get your place sold so you're not paying two mortgages when your new home is finished.

Depending on the builder, they will sometimes agree to delay the start of your home, as long as you've signed a contract and paid your deposit. Or, in some cases they'll agree to take it slow and build your home more slowly than they normally would, and give you an extended closing.

When you're doing this, just make sure it's spelled out extremely clear in your contract, exactly how much time they're giving. A verbal or a handshake agreement here could come back to bite you.

Now, it's up to you to understand how much extra time you want and need going into it. But sometimes this extra padding can be a huge relief. While it's not considered a discount per se, it can save you plenty of stress, worry, aggravation, and ultimately money if you play your cards right.

All right, that does it for negotiating in a seller's market. Now, let's talk about negotiating in a buyer's market. Real estate is cyclical. Whether you're in a seller's market, or a buyer's market right now, it's going to change eventually, so you want to be prepared no matter what stage of the cycle.

Now, just as I enjoyed the easy sales in 2003 and 2004, I also experienced the lowest of the lows in the market around 2007 and 2008. No matter what they tried, builders could not give houses away. So if you were in the market then, you probably got a great deal. But how do you make sure you're getting the best deal you can in a buyer's market? The key is to research what's available in the entire market you're looking in, not just the community you decide is right for you.

What you do is you go around and check out the other communities and see what discounts and incentives other builders are offering. Even if you're not interested in any other community, you take that data and those numbers to the builder and say, "Look, I really like your home and your community, but I'm just not willing to pay more than I should. Here's what I can get for this house down the street."

Now, it's very important when you do that that you make sure you're comparing apples to apples. If the community you're interested in is a gated golf community with a club-house, and a swimming pool, you'll shoot yourself in the foot if you try and compare the home prices there to prices in a community without those amenities.

In most cases, the builder will call your bluff on that. But if you play your cards right, and it's truly a buyer's market, and that builder's struggling to move inventory, you're going to get a great deal.

If the dollar amount of the incentive they offer doesn't quite satisfy you, remember to go after some of the other things we talked about before, like upgrades, lot premiums, and more time to build or an extended closing if you need it.

# CHAPTER 17
# YOUR NEW HOME WALKTHROUGH

The walkthrough, or new home orientation as it is sometimes called, is one of the most important phases in the construction of your new home. It is a time for you to meet with the builder and let him or his representatives acquaint you with your new home and all of its components. The walkthrough is also a time for you to give your new home the once over, looking for any construction issues not up to quality standards.

Here is what could be considered the ideal walkthrough in detail.

**Allow Enough Time**

Allow ample time to go through your new home. In my experience an hour and a half to two hours is sufficient for average sized new homes. Also, leave any pets, kids, or curious friends and relatives at home. There will be plenty of time for them to experience and enjoy your new home in due time. The walkthrough is serious business and should be treated as such. Minimizing distractions is critical.

**What to Bring**

To ensure a successful walkthrough bring along several pens or pencils, a black permanent marker, a packet of neon green dots available at office supply stores, a pad of legal paper, some bottled water, a digital camera (you probably have one on your phone) and a ton of patience. Understand that everything might not be perfect once you start the walk-through. It's just the nature of home building that no matter how careful, the builder can't catch everything. But, if you follow my advice, the builder and his employees will be in the position to get things corrected for you in a timely fashion.

The order of the walkthrough is not really important as long as everything gets covered. As you find items not up to standards, place one of the neon green stickers I suggested you bring on the item and write it down on your legal pad or a punchlist provided by the builder. Then snap a quick picture of the problem. Green dots can mysteriously disappear but if you write it down and take a photo it can't be forgotten for long.

## THINGS TO LOOK FOR

### Breaker Box and Electrical System

You will of course be tempted to head for the front door and bask in the glow of your fresh new home. But not so fast. Let's cover some things in the garage first. The garage houses several important components of your new home and you should become familiar with them. The first item on the list is the breaker box. This is where the electricity that comes into your home is regulated. The walkthrough representative should show you where it is and how to operate it.

Make sure that each breaker has been clearly labeled for you. This will eliminate headaches down the road. Also, there should be some GFI outlets in the garage. Now is a great time for the walkthrough representative to test those in front of you, and to show you how they work. Also, make sure they test the GFI outlets inside the home when you get in there.

### Hot Water Heater

Be sure to check the hot water heater. Make sure the size, measured in gallons, is what you contracted for. The walk-through representative should show you how to turn it off so you will know how to when necessary. There are timers available for your hot water heater that can easily be installed that will save you some money on your electric bills. If your hot water heater comes with a timer, have the walkthrough representative show you how to set it.

### Water Shutoff

The main water shutoff valve to the home will usually be located inside the garage or sometimes on the outside. The walkthrough representative may advise you to turn the water off if you will be leaving the home for days at a time. This is probably good advice, at least initially until you've lived in the home a while and made certain there are no leaky toilets or pipes.

If you do turn off your water, make sure that you also turn

off the breaker for the hot water heater. The hot water heater has coils inside that can burn up if there is no water passing through. When you return home, it is very IMPORTANT to make sure you turn the water back on before turning the hot water heater back on.

### Air Handler and Air Filter

The air handler, which distributes the heated or cooled air throughout your home, will usually be in the garage as well. Make sure the walkthrough representative opens the filter door to show you how to change the air filter. Using the black permanent marker, make note of the filter size in a conspicuous place on the front of the air handler. You should change the air filter about every month for best performance.

### Garage Door

While you're still in the garage, open and close the garage door to check for proper operation and make sure the remote controls work. If your garage door opener came with an outside keypad, ensure that it too works. In the event of a power outage you may need to open the garage door manually. Have the walkthrough representative show you how to do that.

### Kitchen

Once inside the home, the best place to usually start is the kitchen because there is so much to cover there. Make sure that there are no scratches on the kitchen countertops or cabinets. Open and close a random selection of cabinet doors to make sure they are working properly. Make sure the hinges are tight, and the cabinets aren't sticking or rubbing against anything as you are opening and closing them. The representative should give you care and cleaning instructions for both your counters and your cabinets.

Turn on the kitchen faucet and set it to the hottest setting. Here we are checking to make sure that the hot water heater is working properly. As long as you've got hot water after what you feel is a reasonable length of time, you're doing just fine. Have the walkthrough representative show you how the sink disposal works, and how to clear it if it gets clogged. Also have them show you where the individual shutoff valve is for the water in the kitchen as well as the locations of the GFI outlets.

### Appliances

Examine the appliances that came with your home. First, examine the outside of them to make sure there are no scratches or dents. Accidents do happen during construction, but assuming you bought new appliances, and not scratch-and-dent specials, they should be in brand new condition. Turn the stovetop on, check that the burners are working, and then try heating the oven. Assuming everything is working thus far, start the dishwasher to run through a cycle. This is to mainly make sure that there are no leaks in the dishwasher, either when it fills or when it drains.

While the dishwasher is running do a quick check of the refrigerator. If there are integrated ice and or water controls in your refrigerator make sure they work. Don't use the first batch or two of ice; just discard it in the sink. Also, most manufacturers suggest running through and pouring out the first couple of gallons of water from the refrigerator. This is to make sure that the water line becomes clear of any debris that may have gotten inside during construction and installation.

If your home came with a microwave, also check to make sure it works. In the laundry room, start both the washer and the dryer if provided and make sure they are working correctly. Make sure the dryer vent hose is connected.

All of the appliance instructions and warranty information should be kept in one easy-to-access location. Some of them may have cards for you to fill out and mail in to the manufacturer to record your warranty.

### Drywall and Flooring

Before leaving the kitchen, examine the flooring for quality. Also check the walls for any drywall imperfections and check the paint for any spots the painter may have missed. As you see things that don't meet your standards, write them down on the list and place a green dot on or near the problem area. This is so that the drywallers or painters know exactly where to look to correct the problem areas.

Continue your flooring and wall inspection throughout the remainder of the home. Don't forget to look up every now and then and inspect the ceilings.

### Systems and Components

As you are going through the home, have your representative show you how various things work, such as how to set and control the thermostat, how to use the security system and intercom if there is one, and how to operate the central vacuum if you bought one. If your home has a fireplace, whether it is wood burning, gas, or electric, have the walk-through representative show you how it works. Make sure you are given instruction manuals on each of these items and that you place them with your appliance manuals.

**Bathrooms**

Visit the bathrooms and check that the plumbing works. Again turn on the hot water, then the cold water to check the functioning of each. Be sure to check the showers and baths, as well as the sink. Water lines sometimes get reversed. Hot will be cold, and cold will be hot, but this can be easily corrected. Flush the toilets and make sure they have adequate water flow and don't remain running long after you flush. Check the tile work inside the showers to make sure that there are no holes or gaps in the grout or caulking. You don't want water getting behind your tile in there. Examine the vanity tops for scratches and cabinets for loose hinges.

**Exterior**

Be sure to inspect the outside of your home as well. The walkthrough representative should familiarize you with where the hose bibs are located, the sewer cleanout, the A/C unit and anything else that is important. Make sure all of the exterior walls of the home are evenly painted, and do an inspection from ground level of the roof to make sure there are no shingles that look loose or out of place. If your home comes with a sprinkler system, you should be shown how to operate that.

**Warranty**

After you feel you've examined the home top to bottom and have made note of anything that is not satisfactory, you should have the walkthrough representative go over any warranty paperwork that is given to you, so you have an understanding of what items in the home are covered and for how long. Most warranty plans cover most everything for a short period of time, usually the first year. The systems of the home, things like plumbing, electrical, and HVAC, will be covered for a little bit longer, maybe up to two or three years.

There will also be a warranty on the structure. This is the longest lasting component of the warranty. When you hear a builder say a ten-year warranty or 15-year warranty, they are referring to the warranty on the structure. The structure is usually deemed to include the foundation and footings, beams, lintels, columns, walls, roof framing systems and flooring systems.

When things settle down a little bit and you have some time, it can never hurt to read over all of the warranty information. This will help you feel more comfortable with the warranty claim and repair process should you ever need to go through it in the future.

**Emergency Information**

The walkthrough representative will usually give you a list of subcontractors who worked on your home so you can call them if you have a problem with something. You should also be sure that you have a list of repair people to contact should an emergency arise on a weekend or during any non-business hours.

These people should include the heating and A/C contractor should the heat or air break; the electrical contractor if you lose power due to something other than a loss of overall power from the power company; the plumber for if your hot water heater breaks or if there is a sewer stoppage; and finally the number for the roofer if you get a roof leak. I also recommend having the number for a 24-hour water extraction company handy, just in case a pipe breaks or a water heater bursts and your home is flooded.

Write all of these numbers down on one piece of paper and tape them to the in- side of a cabinet so that you can find them easily in an emergency.

**Sign Here Please**

To conclude the walkthrough, the walkthrough representative will typically have paperwork for you to sign stating that he walked you through and familiarized you with everything in the home, and that all the workmanship was satisfactory. Just make sure that the items you found to be unsatisfactory are either on this paperwork or will be attached to it in some form or fashion.

It is not absolutely critical that these items all be completed before your closing, so long as they are documented as needing repair. Invariably in the days and weeks after you move in, you will find more items needing the builder's attention. Just write all these items down as you find them and bring them to the builder's attention.

It has been a long process but now you are all set to enjoy what you have longed for, a beautiful new home!

# CHAPTER 18
# NEW HOME WALKTHROUGH CHECKLIST

U se this checklist during your walkthrough to make sure you don't miss any of the important items I mentioned in the previous chapter.

\_\_\_\_\_ Breaker Box

\_\_\_\_\_ Hot Water Heater

\_\_\_\_\_ Main Water Shutoff

\_\_\_\_\_ Air Handler

\_\_\_\_\_ Garage Door

\_\_\_\_\_ Kitchen

\_\_\_\_\_ Countertops and Cabinets

\_\_\_\_\_ Appliances

\_\_\_\_\_ Water

\_\_\_\_\_ Outlets

\_\_\_\_\_ Drywall and Flooring

\_\_\_\_\_ Systems and Components

\_\_\_\_\_ Thermostat

_____ Security System

_____ Intercom

_____ Central Vac

_____ Bathrooms

_____ Countertops and Cabinets

_____ Tile work

_____ Water

_____ Outlets

_____ Exterior

_____ Hose bibs

_____ Sewer clean-out

_____ Paint

_____ Shingles

_____ Sprinkler System

_____ Pool System

_____ Warranty Paperwork

_____ Emergency Contact Info.


**Additional Notes:**

# CHAPTER 19
## SURVIVING THE MOVE

**M**oving stinks. No matter how good your plan or how many movers you hire, there's no denying the effort it takes to get everything from your old into the right place in your new home. When your plan is to relocate for retirement, there's going to need to be a move involved. There's no way around that. So you might as well embrace it and jump in with a handful of great tricks and tips to help you survive the move.

The first step is to get rid of anything you don't need or want anymore. Everything you sell or donate prior to moving, is one less thing you'll have to pack, move, and unpack.

Go through your entire house with a careful eye and work on getting rid of things you don't want or need anymore. This can dramatically lighten your load on moving day, and simplify your life in the long run.

The next tip for before you start packing, is to take lots of photos so you get a digital inventory of everything that's coming with you on the move.

Also, If you're like most people, your computers and electronics probably involve a maze of different wires and cables that even your tech savvy nephew finds confusing. In order to help you get everything put back together in the right way, make sure that you take a bunch of pictures of how everything is set up before you disassemble it all.

The next tip is to label all your boxes. Just writing what is in a box with a black sharpie is a good start, but you can do even better than that. Expert movers will also identify what room a box should be placed in at the new home. Some will even go so far as to color code the boxes with fluorescent stickers or tape.

In addition to labeling what is in your boxes, and what rooms they belong in, you might also want to label them with numbers to help prioritize which boxes should be unpacked first. Doing this will make it easy to just follow the plan in order as you unpack.

My next tip is don't try to go it alone. Yes, hiring movers can be expensive, but helping with a move is a lot to ask of friends and family, and a frustrating project to take on yourself. Movers bring plenty of experience, and are well worth the cost just in the aggravation they'll save you.

Not being able to find certain things like a toothbrush, medications, or change of clothes after a long day of moving can be frustrating. You definitely want to think ahead and have an overnight bag packed, so you won't be frantically unpacking boxes trying to find the essentials that you need on moving day.

On moving day, a few large pizzas or a few giant subs for your movers will go a long way towards keeping up morale. Stock a cooler or your fridge with plenty of water and Gatorade too. It sounds like such a small thing, but it's a simple gesture that can go a long way.

Moving is the type of project that is very exciting at first, and then slowly grinds on your nerves as the amount of things on your to do list grow faster than you can cross them off.

In order to make sure that you have somewhere to relax when you feel overwhelmed, many experts recommend working to get one room in your new house completely set up as quickly as possible. This will give you somewhere to retreat to when the boxes pile up everywhere else.

Moving is not easy, and it usually isn't very fun. It's a long, frustrating process that takes weeks of planning and then weeks to recover from. However, with these tips, you can make your move a bit easier and hopefully cut back on the amount of aggravation just a bit.

# CHAPTER 20
## THINGS TO DO YOUR FIRST WEEK IN A NEW HOME

Congratulations, you just closed on your new home! Whether you're moving into a brand new home that you just had built or a resale that you fell in love with at first sight, the excitement that follows the closing process never gets old.

The first week in a new house is always the most exciting. But during this exciting time, there are an overwhelming number of things that need to get done in order to get you truly settled into your new home. In order to help with this, I've put together this list of things you're going to want to knock off that to-do list sooner rather than later.

Now if you've built a new home this one shouldn't be too much of an issue. During the construction process your home has probably been on what's called a builder's key, but on the day of your closing the building superintendent will typically change those locks out and give you the only set of keys at your closing.

But if you're buying a resale, one of the very first things that you need to do before spending the night in your new house is make sure that no one else is going to have access, which means that you're going to want to change the locks and any passcode entries like you might have for the garage door. Just to be safe, you should also be sure to change the codes for the remote garage door openers.

Fair warning, getting all of the utilities into your name is definitely going to be a hassle. No one likes dealing with the utility companies, but it has to get done, so get it over with as soon as possible, preferably on the same day as your closing. On the bright side, at least when you're through you'll have internet and cable TV.

If your new home qualifies for a homestead exemption, you're absolutely going to want to get that filed before you forget about it. As you probably know, homestead exemptions can mean significant savings on property taxes, but in most cases they are time sensitive, meaning you typically have to file for them by a certain date in order to get the benefits.

Because it doesn't seem as urgent as some of the other tasks on this list, this one is easy to put off. But I'm warning you that if you do that, chances are you forget about this completely and you'll be kicking yourself later. Just get it done.

This is a no brainer when buying a resale, but even if you are moving into a brand new home, you're still going to want to clean the place before you start to get comfortable. When buying a brand new home, you'll get what's called a construction clean right before your walk through and closing.

In my experience, most homes still need a little TLC after that if you know what I mean. Plus, cleaning things likes shelves and drawers is a whole lot easier to do before you fill them with all your stuff. So again, don't let yourself procrastinate on this one.

A new house never really feels like home until you change the color in a few of the rooms. If you're moving into a brand new house where everything is probably white because a lot of builders won't entertain special paint color requests, you're definitely going to want to introduce some color.

Just like with cleaning, painting is a whole lot easier in an empty room than one that is filled with furniture. So you should definitely focus on painting whatever rooms you might be planning on painting before you start moving your things in.

Having closets and drawers that are well organized starts with great planning from day one. If you want to make sure your closets and drawers are well organized for years to come, either get out to your local home improvement store and invest in some organizing systems during the first week in your new house, or call somebody in, like a California Closets, before those closets and drawers start acquiring all your stuff.

You're eventually going to meet the neighbors one way or another, but if you don't meet them during your first week it becomes easy to keep putting it off until you reach the point where things get a little weird. Even if you aren't an overly outgoing person, a simple "Hi, I'm Ryan," during your first week can go a long way towards having a good relationship with your neighbors for years to come.

Let's be honest, this is a big list and we are really just scratching the surface of everything that needs to get done as you begin to settle into your new home. Don't let yourself forget that this is supposed to be fun. Take a few minutes every once in a while to relax and appreciate your new home.

# CHAPTER 21
## GETTING TO KNOW YOUR NEW COMMUNITY

Hopefully by now you've moved into the home of your dreams, in the perfect community for you and your family. The next step is to get know your new community and you're gonna want to acclimated fast. No one likes to feel like the new person in town, so you want to get to know your new surroundings quickly.

A lot of communities nowadays have monthly or quarterly new resident socials, where new residents can get to know each other as well as some of the other residents who've been in the community a little or even a lot longer. This is a great opportunity for you to meet and mingle with other people who are in the same boat as you are in a new environment and new surroundings.

But, if you don't want to wait or if your new community doesn't have a new resident event in place, here are some other great ways to meet people and get yourself more familiar with your new community. The best way to feel more comfortable in your new community is to start making new friends as soon as possible.

The easiest way to make friends with your new neighbors is to invite them over for dinner. You can have a few neighbors over for a backyard barbecue, order a bunch of extra large pizzas, or actually put that fancy new kitchen of yours to work. They type of food involved is a minimal concern compared to the act of attempting to get to know the people you now share a neighborhood with.

Depending on what type of community you choose, there are likely a number of leagues, organizations, groups, or clubs you could join to get to know other people. The people you meet through your hobbies and other leisure activities will generally become some of your best friends in your new community.

So get started on building those connections as soon as possible. Similarly, almost every community is going to have some great charitable causes and almost everyone of those causes would love some new blood to come in and lend a helping hand. You won't have to look further than the local paper, community center, or and church, to find a great organization where you can volunteer your time. Not only will your help benefit the cause, you will also make lots of new friends in the process.

I'll leave the debate between coffee and beer up to you, but if you show up at a local coffee shop a few times and then start talking to the person making your drink, you will have a handful of new friends and learn an awful lot about the community in no time. Baristas and bartenders can be a great source of information for anyone who is new to a community. They interact with many of your neighbors on a daily basis, and generally have a good feel for the pulse of a community.

This is how we all learned our way around a new town in the old days, we got lost. Leave your GPS at home and head out for a drive around town. When you get lost, just let your gut tell you where you should go and see where you end up.

The concept of driving around a community without directions will allow you to really get a feel for what the town looks like, and you might even discover some interesting places just off the beaten path.

At least in the early going, the local newspaper can be a tremendous help in getting to know your new community and the local area. Eventually, you might decide you want to go paperless and just check out the online version if they have one, but in the beginning, when you're new to the area, I think you should go ahead and get the printed version and read it each day.

Another great way to learn more about the things that are happening in your new community, is to go to a city council or homeowners association meeting. This will immediately put you on the radar of the decision makers in the community and it can also help you understand the current issues in the community, and the plans for the future.

You might be new in town today, but that doesn't mean you have to be new in town tomorrow. The sooner you get out and get to know your community, the sooner it will truly feel like home.